PEANUT BUTTER PUPPIES

GREG MURRAY

GIBBS SMITH
TO ENRICH AND INSPIRE HUMANKIND

First Edition
25 24 23 22 21 5 4 3 2 1
Text and photographs © 2021 Greg Murray

Published by
Gibbs Smith
P.O. Box 667
Layton, Utah 84041

1.800.835.4993 orders
www.gibbs-smith.com

Designed by Tracy Sunrize Johnson
Gibbs Smith books are printed on paper produced from sustainable PEFC-
certified forest/controlled wood source. Learn more at www.pefc.org.
Printed and bound in China

Library of Congress Control Number: 2020941999
ISBN: 978-1-4236-5659-3

Dedicated to

RESCUE VOLUNTEERS AND STAFF

who work tirelessly to save the lives of

ANIMALS AROUND THE WORLD.

CONTENTS

INTRODUCTION

IN EARLY 2014, I began taking photos of Bailey, our rescued cane corso, eating peanut butter. I wanted to capture more animated photos of her because her droopy jowls sometimes made her appear a little sad. More than a year later, I began photographing dogs in my studio eating peanut butter. I thought a photo series would be fun and keep me busy during my slow season in January and February. I posted a gallery of the photos online and, just like that, it went viral: selected photos were featured online and in newspapers around the world. Long story short, I signed a book deal and my first book, *Peanut Butter Dogs*, was released in 2017.

Nothing made me happier than to know people around the world were smiling and laughing because of my photos of dogs enjoying peanut butter. The ability to create something that brings joy to others is an unbelievably good feeling. While I thought I was set on only doing one book about dogs eating peanut butter, I was also eager to bring more joy, smiles, and laughter to the world. Three years later, in 2020, it only seemed fitting to make another peanut butter book.

For the original *Peanut Butter Dogs* book, I photographed more than 140 dogs in about a three-month period. It was quite the whirlwind! While it was easy to find models (who wouldn't want their dog in a book?), it was difficult to photograph so many in a short period of time while simultaneously photographing animals for my regular pet-photography clients. When it came to *Peanut Butter Puppies*, I had more time and only had to photograph about seventy dogs. (Kind of sounds funny saying, "I *only* had to photograph about seventy dogs," and do it during a pandemic!) My goal for this book was to photograph a wide variety of mutts and breed-specific rescue puppies. About every three weeks, I posted a model call on my Facebook page, which provided me more than enough puppies to choose from. Some of the puppies were being fostered or were in the shelter when I photographed them and now are in loving forever homes. Some of these puppies were adopted during the pandemic to first-time dog owners looking for a furry companion to be part of their home. It was fun to work with first-time dog owners who were still navigating the world of puppyhood. I enjoyed offering advice, answering questions, and seeing their love for their new family member.

I chose to photograph only rescue dogs for *Peanut Butter Puppies* to help bring continued awareness to the importance of pet adoption. To save an animal's life is an amazing privilege. Beginning here, and moving forward, I have committed to only featuring rescue animals in any of my books. Millions of dogs and cats enter shelters and rescue organizations every year—puppies, kittens, aging seniors, and all ages in between. They need us, not only to adopt them but also to advocate, educate, volunteer, donate, sponsor, and foster on their behalf.

Together, let's continue to make a difference and decrease the number of homeless animals. If you haven't done so already, please consider saving a life next time you are ready to welcome a pet into your home. You will not regret it.

—*GREG MURRAY*

ARCHIE
7 months
Chihuahua

AURORA
6 months
Bernese mountain dog/poodle mix

COLBY & CHEDDAR
5 months
Australian cattle dogs

ZOLA
8 weeks
Pit bull mix

SCARLETT
10 months
Saint Bernard

MUTTON
9 weeks
Pit bull mix

SCOUT
1 year
Dachshund

ARLO
4 months
Doberman pinscher

FIONA WIGGLESWORTH
8 months
Boston terrier

ZOEY
9 months
Mastiff mix

WALLABY
7 months
Blue heeler

31

CALI
5 months
Pit bull mix

TORI
8 months
Doberman mix

BODHI
11 months
Catahoula/pit bull mix

BEAN
7 months
Labrador retriever/boxer mix

YOGI & TULLY
10 weeks
Pit bull mixes

GINNIE
10 weeks
Chihuahua mix

DAISY
5 months
Pit bull/beagle mix

DODGER
5 months
Pit bull/beagle mix

REED
6 months
Corgi/terrier/miniature pinscher mix

RIVER & BUCK
8 weeks
Hound mixes

DOLLY
7 months
Beagle mix

CROWLER
7 months
Pit bull mix

RUFUS
5 months
Great Dane mix

GRETA
3 months
Great Pyrenees/
German shepherd mix

RANGER
8 months
Beagle mix

SOPHIE
10 months
Pit bull mix

BUGG
5 months
Shepherd/retriever mix

HOWIE
10 weeks
Beagle/border collie mix

QUINT
1 year
Dalmatian

ZIA
6 months
Great Pyrenees mix

BAILEY
5 months
Pit bull mix

MILLIE
6 months
Cocker spaniel/
Chihuahua/pug mix

MAGGIE
7 months
Shepherd mix

NESSA
8 months
Pit bull mix

LUCY
5 months
King Charles cavalier/
hound mix

ECHO
4 months
Boxer mix

SUNNY
10 months
Pit bull mix

COOPER
3 months
Beagle/dachshund mix

HARLEY
1 year
Pit bull mix

BELLE
6 months
Cocker spaniel

ROSCOE
7 months
Shepherd/hound mix

SHELDON
1 year
Shetland sheepdog/
pit bull mix

LILY
1 year
Dachshund

BUMBLE
10 months
Beagle/bulldog mix

EVE
6 months
Great Dane

THALIA
3 months
Beagle/shepherd mix

GINNY
7 months
Golden retriever

CHUMP
9 weeks
Pit bull mix

SEAMUS
3 months
Labrador retriever/
pit bull mix

MILLIE GRACE
5 months
Pit bull/mastiff mix

FREYA
5 months
American bulldog mix

OCIE
6 months
Pit bull/shar-pei mix

CHUBBS
8 months
Labrador retriever mix

ZION
6 months
Pit bull/border collie mix

MORCHELLA
8 months
Pekingese/Jack Russell terrier mix

RUPERT
4 months
Pit bull mix

DINKERS
7 months
Shih tzu mix

PENNY LANE
4 months
"Red heeler" Australian cattle dog mix

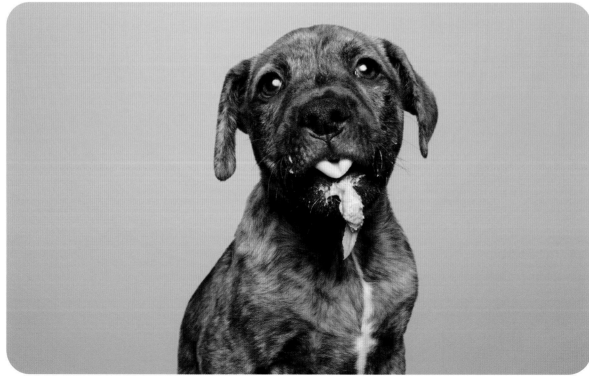

CAT & NICKS
8 weeks
Labrador/pit bull mixes

PERRY
8 weeks
Labrador/pit bull mix

BULLET
5 months
German shepherd mix

LUNA
6 months
Cane corso

RORY PICKLES
1 year
Pit bull mix

ROXY
6 months
Pit bull mix

WILLETT & LILY
4 months
Saint Bernard/retriever mixes

DISCLAIMER

Please note the following about dogs and peanut butter before you consider giving it to a furry friend of yours:

In most cases, a little bit of peanut butter is perfectly fine for dogs. It's generally safe, and it's even a good source of protein, vitamins, and healthy fats.

Too much of anything, including peanut butter, is not good for dogs. The puppies in this book were only given small amounts of peanut butter during photo shoots.

All-natural peanut butter, made up of peanuts and salt, is ideal. Avoid any peanut butter that contains xylitol. Xylitol can be very dangerous to dogs. ALWAYS check labels before giving any type of food to your dog.

Consider consulting your veterinarian prior to giving peanut butter to your dog(s). Just like with humans, a few dogs may have peanut allergies even though most dogs have no problems with peanuts. If your dog appears to have a bad reaction to eating peanuts at any time, contact your vet immediately.

ACKNOWLEDGMENTS

Thank you to everyone who brought in their
amazing rescue puppies to be part of this book.
Thank you to my family, especially Kristen,
Evie, Leo, and Kensie.

LEO & KENSIE

140

© Kayla Lupean

ABOUT THE AUTHOR

Greg Murray is a commercial, lifestyle, and portrait animal photographer based out of Cleveland, Ohio. After getting his degree in business from Loyola University Chicago and spending ten years in the corporate world as an HR professional, Greg left the field and followed his dream of becoming a full-time pet photographer. He is the author/photographer of *Peanut Butter Dogs* (2017) and *Pit Bull Heroes: 49 Underdogs with Resilience & Heart* (2019). Greg is a rescue animal and pit bull–type dog advocate who in 2018, along with many more dedicated advocates, helped to end a ten-year ban on pit bull–type dogs in his hometown of Lakewood, Ohio. He lives in Lakewood with his wife, Kristen, their daughter, Evie, and their two rescue dogs, Leo and Kensie.

@thegregmurray | Greg Murray Photography | www.gmurrayphoto.com

ALSO AVAILABLE,
WHEREVER BOOKS ARE SOLD!

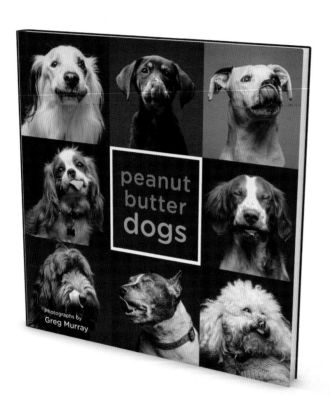

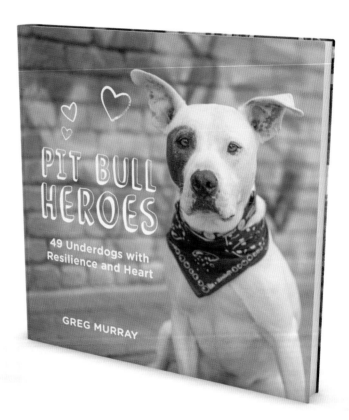